# Things to Know
# When Interviewing
# for a Fundraiser Job

First published by Kjøller 2023

## Disclaimer:

The information contained in this book is provided for general informational purposes only. While every effort has been made to ensure that the information is accurate and up-to-date, The Author makes no representations or warranties of any kind, express or implied, about the completeness, accuracy, reliability, suitability, or availability with respect to the information, products, services, or related graphics contained in the book for any purpose.

The Author disclaims any liability for any loss or damage, including without limitation, indirect or consequential loss or damage, or any loss or damage whatsoever arising from loss of data or profits arising out of, or in connection with, the use of this book.

Readers are solely responsible for determining the appropriateness of the information contained in this book for their specific purposes and should seek professional advice before acting upon any information contained herein. The Author shall not be liable for any damages of any kind arising from the use of this book or the information contained herein.

# Table of Contents

# Introduction

Looking for a job in fundraising can be an exhilarating and challenging experience. However, once you start the application process, you realize the intimidating amount of jargon being used. With so many complicated terms and definitions, it can be overwhelming to keep up with the lingo.

If you feel like you're drowning in the vocabulary of the non-profit sector, fear not. This book contains a comprehensive glossary of key terms that are commonly used in the fundraising job interview process. From PAR to CFR to LYBUNT, you'll be able to decipher what these terms mean and how to apply them to your interview questions.

By having a better understanding of these concepts, you'll be able to impress your interviewer and show that you have a strong foundation in the world of fundraising. So whether you're a fresh graduate or a seasoned professional, this resource will serve as your personal decoder to navigate the jargon-filled waters of the fundraising job market.

# 10

Inclusivity

## Acknowledgement

Acknowledgements are thank-you messages sent to donors after they have made a contribution. It is important for fundraisers to understand the importance of timely and well-crafted acknowledgement letters, as they are essential in building relationships with donors and encouraging future giving.

## Advancement

Advancement refers to the overall strategy and tactics used to build lasting relationships with donors to raise funds for a nonprofit organization. This includes annual giving, major gifts, planned giving, and stewardship. Understanding how to devise and execute a successful advancement plan is essential to raising funds and growing an organization's donor base.

## Allocation

Allocation refers to the process of distributing funds within an organization, such as directing donations toward specific programs or initiatives. Understanding how to allocate funds effectively is important when working in a fundraiser job, as it can impact an organization's ability to fulfill its mission, retain donors, and demonstrate financial responsibility.

## Analytics

Analytics refers to the process of using data to better understand donor behavior and to identify patterns in giving. Knowing how to analyze and interpret data is critical when developing fundraising strategies and measuring the effectiveness of campaigns.

## Annual Fund

An annual fund is a year-round effort to attract donations from individuals, corporations, and foundations. These funds support the organization's ongoing programs and operations. Understanding how to properly manage and cultivate relationships with donors is important when working on an annual fund as a fundraiser.

# Annual Giving Program

An annual giving program is a year-round effort to attract donations from individuals, corporations, and foundations to support an organization's ongoing programs and operations. Understanding how to effectively market to and engage donors through an annual giving program is crucial when working in a fundraiser job.

# Appeal

A fundraising appeal is a written or spoken request for a donation. It is important to know the difference between the types of appeals, including direct mail, email, and social media. Understanding how to construct an effective appeal is crucial in a fundraiser job, as it is often the first point of contact with prospective donors.

# Appeals Board

An appeals board is a group of volunteers or staff that reviews appeals from donors who wish to dispute a decision made by the organization. It is important for fundraisers to understand the appeals process to ensure that donors feel heard and appreciated, which can lead to future giving.

## Asset-based fundraising

Asset-based fundraising involves soliciting donations of stocks, bonds, and other financial assets, rather than cash donations. Learning about asset-based fundraising strategies can be helpful for fundraisers looking to diversify their organization's donor base and revenue streams.

## Association of Fundraising Professionals (AFP)

The Association of Fundraising Professionals is a professional organization for fundraisers that offers training and networking opportunities, as well as a code of ethical principles that must be followed by all members. Familiarizing oneself with these principles can help ensure ethical fundraising practices.

## Cultivation

The process of building relationships with potential donors through personalized communication and engagement strategies.

## Donor Relations

Establishing and maintaining positive relationships with potential and existing donors to ensure ongoing support for the organization's fundraising efforts.

## Event Fundraising

A strategy that involves organizing and promoting fundraising events, such as galas, auctions, or charity runs, to raise money for the organization.

## Fundraising Metrics

A set of performance indicators used to measure the effectiveness of fundraising efforts, such as donor retention rates, average gift size, and return on investment.

## Grant Writing

The process of researching, writing, and submitting grant proposals to secure funding from foundations, government agencies, or other organizations.

## Health Marketplace

The health marketplace is a fundraising strategy that partners with healthcare providers who refer their clients to nonprofit organizations. Fundraisers should know and form good relationships with healthcare professionals who can refer their patients and clients to the nonprofit organizations.

# Heirloom Gift

An heirloom gift is a gift that has been handed down from generation to generation in a family. When interviewing for a fundraising job, it's important to understand how to build and cultivate relationships with donors to the point that they feel comfortable giving their heirloom gifts. Heirloom gifts are unique and rare, so they can be used to garner a lot of attention and support for nonprofit organizations.

# Heritage-Related Accounts

Heritage-related accounts are accounts that are established to support causes that are dear to a person's heart. People are more inclined to donate money when it is in support of a personal interest or connection, and fundraisers should be aware of how to find and target these heritage-related accounts.

# Hierarchy of Communication

The hierarchy of communication is a ranking of communication methods that are effective in fundraising. It involves providing potential donors with information through various media channels such as social media and email. When interviewing for a fundraising job, it is important to know how to approach each level of media with a unique message.

# Hierarchy of Giving

The hierarchy of giving is a ranking of types of donations, ranging from small gifts to large ones. It's important to understand the hierarchy of giving when interviewing for a fundraiser job since it helps in creating fundraising strategies. A fundraiser should focus on the higher end of the hierarchy, as large donations make up the bulk of fundraising.

# Honorarium

An honorarium is a fee paid for professional services that are usually provided by an expert in a field or an accomplished individual. When interviewing for a fundraising job, it's important to be aware of the various ways in which an honorarium can be used to attract larger donations, foster relationships with donors and professionals, and make events more successful.

# Hospitals and Healthcare Facilities

Hospitals and healthcare facilities are prime spots for fundraisers to solicit donations. Hospitals rely heavily on donations and they are more than willing to open their doors to fundraisers. When interviewing for a fundraising job, it's important to understand how and when to approach hospitals and healthcare facilities for optimum results.

## House Parties

House parties are informal events that involve inviting donors to a house or other venue for entertainment and socializing. This is a fundraising strategy that allows individuals to show their support for a cause without making a large commitment. A fundraiser should be able to organize, plan and execute house parties skillfully to maximize the potential for donations.

## Hoverer

A hoverer in fundraising refers to a person who does not make a firm commitment to donate, but instead hovers around the decision. It's important for a fundraiser to know how to deal with a hoverer, since their readiness to donate is often unclear. Strategies to handle hoverers include building rapport, being persistent, and providing more information.

## Humane Treatment

When soliciting donations, fundraising professionals should apply humane, ethical, and moral principles in their dealings with donors. They should ensure that all donor information is kept confidential, give back to the community through charitable causes and also ensure that donors feel respected and appreciated. As a result, donors will be more likely to continue giving and support the organization.

# Impact

The measurable difference that a fundraising campaign or initiative has on the organization's mission and beneficiaries. Fundraising is all about creating a positive impact, and therefore, it is crucial to understand the concept of impact and how to measure it when applying for a fundraising job.

# Impact Investing

Allocating funds to organizations with the intent of creating positive social or environmental change while also generating financial returns. Understanding the importance and concepts of impact investing can be valuable when interviewing for a job in a more specialized fundraising field.

# Incentives

Rewards or benefits offered to donors or supporters to encourage them to contribute more. The ability to create creative incentives can be a valuable skill when interviewing for a fundraiser job as it can help motivate donors to give more while also building loyalty.

# Inclusion

Embracing diversity and ensuring all individuals, regardless of race, gender, or other characteristics, feel valued and included. As fundraisers work with a broad range of donors and supporters, it is crucial to demonstrate a commitment to diversity and inclusion when interviewing for a job in the sector.

# In-Kind donations

Non-monetary gifts or services given to the organization, such as goods or volunteer time. When interviewing for a fundraiser position, it is crucial to have a clear understanding of in-kind donations and how they can impact the organization's budget and goals.

# Innovation

The ability to develop new and creative ideas to improve fundraising efforts and generate more support. Fundraising is an ever-evolving field, and therefore, it is essential to display a willingness to be innovative and adapt to new challenges when interviewing for a job in this sector.

# Integrity

Upholding honesty and ethical behavior in all aspects of the job. Fundraisers often handle sensitive information, such as financial data and donor details, and therefore, must maintain a high level of integrity in their work. Demonstrating a commitment to ethical practices and transparency can be important during the interview process.

# Intermediary Organizations

Non-Profit organizations that act as intermediaries between donors and other non-profit organizations in need of funding. When interviewing for a job in the sector, knowledge of intermediary organizations and their role in the fundraising ecosystem can be valuable.

# Interpersonal Skills

The ability to communicate and interact with others effectively, including active listening, empathy, and persuasion. When interviewing for a fundraiser job, it is essential to display strong interpersonal skills as the role involves building relationships with potential donors, creating partnerships with other organizations, and collaborating with colleagues.

# Investment

The act of committing resources, including time, money, or energy, to support a cause or organization. Understanding the concept of investment can be essential when applying for a fundraising job, where the role involves convincing donors to invest in the organization's mission and the impact it creates.

# Key Donor

A key donor is an individual or organization that makes substantial donations to a charitable cause. Fundraisers may seek to cultivate relationships with key donors to increase their likelihood of making future contributions.

# Key Messaging

Key messaging refers to the core messages that fundraisers want to convey to potential donors. These messages should be tailored to the organization's mission, values, and goals, and should be communicated consistently across all channels.

# Key Performance Area

A key performance area is a specific focus area within a fundraising campaign that is critical to achieving its goals. Examples may include donor acquisition, retention, engagement, or upgrading. Understanding key performance areas can help fundraisers allocate resources effectively and make data-driven decisions.

# Key Performance Driver

A key performance driver is an element that strongly influences the success of a fundraising campaign. Examples may include the quality of the organization's messaging, the effectiveness of its marketing strategies, or the strength of its donor relationships.

# Key Relationships

Key relationships refer to the partnerships and collaborations that fundraisers develop with stakeholders such as board members, volunteers, and corporate sponsors. Strong relationships can help fundraisers build trust, leverage resources, and expand their networks.

# Kick-off Meeting

A kick-off meeting is a gathering of stakeholders to initiate a fundraising campaign or project. The purpose of the meeting is to outline goals, discuss roles and responsibilities, and establish timelines for the project.

# Know Your Customer (KYC)

Know your customer (KYC) refers to the process of verifying the identity of donors and their financial information. This information can help fundraisers identify potential donors, develop tailored marketing campaigns, and ensure compliance with regulatory requirements.

# Knowledge Management

Knowledge management refers to the process of capturing, storing, and sharing information within an organization. For fundraisers, this may involve tracking donor information, developing fundraising strategies based on previous successes, and sharing best practices with colleagues.

# KPI

Key performance indicators are metrics used to measure the effectiveness of a fundraiser's efforts. Common KPIs may include the number of donations received, dollar amount of funds raised, and the percent increase in donor retention. Understanding KPIs can help fundraisers set goals and evaluate their performance.

# KPI Dashboard

A KPI dashboard is a tool that displays key performance indicators in a visual format, allowing fundraisers to quickly assess their progress towards meeting their goals.

# Landing page

A web page specifically designed to capture leads or donations from potential donors. Landing pages typically have minimal navigation options and include a clear call-to-action. Creating effective landing pages can be crucial for fundraising campaigns, as they can help convert interested individuals into donors.

# Lapsed donor

A donor who used to donate to an organization or cause but has not done so in a significant amount of time. Re-engaging lapsed donors can be a cost-effective way to increase funds raised. It's important to identify the reasons why a donor stopped donating and to create targeted messaging that speaks to their motivations.

# Last-minute donor outreach

Reaching out to potential donors in the final days or hours of a campaign to encourage a final donation. Last-minute donor outreach can be a stressful but potentially fruitful aspect of fundraising campaigns. It's important to have a clear call-to-action and a sense of urgency to motivate donors to give.

# Lead donor

An individual, group or organization that donates a significant amount of money, often the largest donation, to a particular cause or campaign. Knowing how to identify and cultivate lead donors can be essential for fundraisers looking to meet or exceed their fundraising goals.

# Legacy giving

A type of fundraising where donors leave a gift to an organization or cause in their will. Legacy giving is often promoted as a way for donors to leave a lasting impact and can be a valuable source of long-term support for fundraisers. Knowing how to create effective messaging around legacy giving and how to approach potential donors about legacy gifts can be crucial for fundraisers.

# Letter of intent

A document that outlines a fundraiser's plans for a campaign. It typically includes information such as the campaign's timeline, budget, and goals. A letter of intent can be used to pitch a campaign to potential donors, sponsors, or partners. It's important to be clear and detailed in a letter of intent, as it serves as an introduction to the campaign.

# LinkedIn outreach

Reaching out to potential donors or partners through LinkedIn, a social media platform primarily designed for professional networking. LinkedIn outreach can be an effective way to connect with individuals or organizations that may be interested in supporting a campaign. It's important to personalize outreach messages and have a clear message about the campaign in order to be successful.

## List segmentation

The practice of dividing an organization's donor list into sub-groups based on demographics, past giving behavior, or other relevant factors. Segmenting a list allows fundraisers to create targeted messaging that speaks to each group's motivations and desires. This can lead to more successful fundraising campaigns and increased engagement from donors.

## Livestream fundraising

A type of online fundraising where a content creator or organization hosts a live stream event and asks viewers to donate during the broadcast. Livestream fundraising can be a highly effective way to engage donors, especially younger generations who are more likely to consume content online.

## Long-term donor cultivation

The process of building and maintaining strong relationships with donors over a period of time. Cultivating long-term donor relationships can lead to increased giving, continued participation in campaigns, and referrals to other potential donors. It's important to personalize communication with donors, offer engagement opportunities, and show appreciation for their contributions in order to cultivate strong long-term relationships.

## Major Gifts

Large donations typically received from a single donor, foundation or corporation in support of a specific project or program.

## Naming rights

The ability of a donor to name a facility, program, or event after themselves or someone else they wish to honor. Fundraisers must understand the value and impact of naming rights and be able to negotiate them effectively.

## National fundraising campaigns

Large-scale fundraising efforts that are run nationwide, such as United Way or the American Cancer Society. Fundraisers should be familiar with national campaigns that may impact their organization's fundraising success.

## Needs assessment

An evaluation of an organization's fundraising needs that includes an analysis of current and potential donor bases, as well as an assessment of fundraising strategies and tactics. Understanding the results of a needs assessment can help fundraisers develop effective fundraising plans.

# Net revenue

The total revenue generated by a fundraising campaign minus any expenses incurred. Understanding net revenue is necessary for assessing the success of a fundraising campaign and analyzing future fundraising plans.

# Networking

Building relationships with potential donors, sponsors, and partners to increase fundraising opportunities. This involves attending events, reaching out to contacts, and being active on social media platforms to expand an organization's reach.

# Niche

A specific area of fundraising focus, such as healthcare, education, or environmental causes. Knowing an organization's niche is crucial for fundraisers as it helps them identify potential donors and tailor their approach to match the organization's focus.

# Non-governmental organizations (NGOs)

Organizations that operate without government control and typically focus on humanitarian, environmental, or social issues. Fundraisers must be knowledgeable about various NGOs and their specific fundraising practices.

# Non-monetary donations

Contributions to an organization that are not in the form of money, such as volunteer time, goods, or services. Fundraisers need to be knowledgeable about other ways donors can contribute and how to properly handle such donations.

# Non-profit sector

Organizations that do not operate for profit and focus on a social cause, aiming to improve society in some way. This includes charities, foundations, and advocacy groups.

# Not-for-profit

Refers to organizations that operate with a goal of achieving a social cause, rather than generating profit. This term can be used interchangeably with "non-profit," but it emphasizes the idea that the organization is not focused on financial gain. Fundraisers must be familiar with the not-for-profit sector to effectively raise funds for their organizations.

# Objections

Reasons that potential donors may have for not donating. These can include concerns about the organization's mission, skepticism about the impact of their donation, or financial constraints. Being able to overcome objections and persuade donors to give is a critical skill for any fundraiser.

# Objectives

The goals that an organization wants to achieve through fundraising efforts. These may include financial targets, specific programs or initiatives, or long-term strategic vision. It's essential to understand the objectives of the nonprofit you'll be working for before starting any fundraising efforts, as this will help you tailor your approach to meet their specific needs and goals.

# Offering

The specific ask that you make of donors or supporters. This may include asking for a specific dollar amount or inviting people to attend an event, sign up for a mailing list or volunteer. Understanding how to craft an effective offering is critical to persuading people to give.

# Online fundraising

The process of raising money through online channels, such as social media or crowdfunding platforms. Understanding how to leverage online tools for fundraising is becoming increasingly important, as more and more donors are giving through digital channels.

# Operating budget

The financial plan that outlines an organization's expenses and revenue streams. Understanding the operating budget is essential for fundraisers, as it helps you understand how your fundraising efforts fit into the overall financial picture of the nonprofit.

# Opportunity cost

The cost of choosing one course of action over another. In fundraising, opportunity cost often refers to the potential revenue that could have been generated if the organization had invested in a different fundraising strategy. Understanding opportunity cost is key to making strategic decisions about fundraising efforts.

# Organizational culture

The shared values, beliefs, and practices that define an organization's identity. Understanding the culture of the nonprofit you'll be working for is key to being an effective fundraiser, as it will help you build relationships and communicate more effectively with supporters.

# Outcomes

The specific results that an organization hopes to achieve through their fundraising efforts. These may include financial goals, as well as specific programmatic or impact-related outcomes. Understanding the desired outcomes of fundraising efforts is key to setting goals and measuring success.

# Outreach

The process of reaching out to potential donors or supporters, often through events or direct communication. Outreach is a critical part of any fundraising job, as it's essential to build relationships with current and potential supporters to help grow your organization's donor base.

# Overhead costs

The indirect expenses associated with running a nonprofit organization, such as rent, utilities, and administrative salaries. Donors may be hesitant to give if they feel like too much of their donation will go towards overhead, so understanding how to effectively communicate the importance of overhead costs is essential for fundraisers.

# Planned Giving

A strategy that involves incorporating donations into a donor's overall financial and estate planning, typically through bequests or charitable trusts.

# Prospect Research

The process of identifying potential donors based on their giving history, philanthropic interests, and personal connections to the organization.

# Reach

A measurement of the number of potential donors or supporters that fundraisers can reach through their digital and social media presence, traditional PR and marketing strategies, and networking events. Amplifying your message across a variety of channels can make your organization's mission known and accessible to a larger audience.

# Relationship Management

This skill is key for fundraisers as it involves developing and maintaining relationships with donors and supporters. Relationship management involves being organized, timely, communicative, attentive, and adjusting your communication style to fit each donor.

# Reporting

Keeping track of fundraising figures, donor data and other relevant metrics, fundraisers should be able to create and deliver informative reports to management and stakeholders.

## Research

Conducting research on potential donors, corporate partnerships, and funding opportunities can contribute to a successful fundraising campaign. Information gathering through tools, such as prospect research software or consultants are crucial for research success.

## Return on Investment

Also known as ROI, this is a measure of the effectiveness of fundraising campaigns. ROI can be calculated by subtracting the total costs of a fundraising campaign from the funds received, divided by the cost of the campaign. Understanding and maximizing your organization's ROI is important for long-term fundraising success.

## Revenue Streams

The multiple funding sources that a nonprofit relies on to meet its financial needs. Understanding the revenue streams of the organization you're fundraising for will help you better determine which donors and fundraising methods are most appropriate.

# Solicitation

The act of requesting financial contributions, whether from individuals, corporations, or foundations. Solicitation can take on many forms and approaches such as annual giving campaigns, grant applications, planned giving strategies among others.

# Stewardship

The ongoing process of thanking and recognizing donors for their contributions and keeping them informed about how their donation is making a difference.

# Strategic Planning

Developing a strategic plan is essential for all fundraising efforts. This plan is a step-by-step guide that outlines the goals, action items, timeline, and financial goals of the campaign.

# Teamwork

Effective fundraisers recognize that collaboration with their colleagues and other departments in the nonprofit organization is essential to achieving fundraising goals. Working as a team and supporting each other's efforts strengthens the organization's overall efforts to achieve the mission.

# There are simply no topic-specific terms that start with the letter "X". However, I can provide a list of relevant terms that start with other letters

## Understanding ethical fundraising

Ethical fundraising involves fundraising with a moral and legal approach. It primarily focuses on complete transparency with regard to the fund allocation and utilization. Ethical fundraising is to be practiced to maximize contributions from donors and to foster long-lasting relationships between the organization and the donors. It is the candidate's responsibility to be thoroughly informed about various ethical fundraising techniques, approaches, and compliance requirements during the interview stage.

# Understanding event management

Event management is another essential aspect of fundraising, involving fundraising plans, logistics, and marketing. Ensure that the candidate understands the internal processes of organizing events for fundraising campaigns, from pre-event promotion to scheduling, protocols, and strategies.

# Understanding of the organization's mission

Understanding the non-profit organization's purpose is crucial when interviewing for a fundraisor job. Before the interview, research the organization's mission statement and understand its purpose, as it will help you communicate your passion for contributing towards the cause its supporting. This knowledge will also help you answer how to represent the organization in a fundraising campaign.

# Undertaking research

Undertaking market research is pivotal to know the prospective donors and their approach towards fundraising. Research will help the candidate understand more about the competition, which will eventually help in setting a clear fundraising goal that aligns with the donor's expectations.

## Unique Selling Point

The unique point of the non-profit organization must be clearly stated in the interview. The unique selling point helps the candidate to convince the organization of an effective fundraising department/skillset. Present the fundraising strategies or methods that differentiate the organization from other competitors and how it can attract fundraising.

## Unrelentless targeting

Fundraising jobs require constant efforts to acquire donors. Thus, the candidate must be persistent in targeting the prospective donors constantly. They must have an undying energy and spirit to understand that maintaining momentum of a fundraising operation will lead to success.

## Urgency

To thrive in this sector, the candidate needs to have a sense of urgency. It means having the ability to work within deadlines and amicably adapting to unexpexted scenarios.

## Used technology

Understanding the technology used for fundraising is imperative when interviewing for the role. Develop working knowledge over online fundraising platforms, social media, email marketing campaigns, and CRM systems. The use of a fundraising software serves as a helpful tool in maximizing productivity and fundraising efficiency.

## Using communication skills

A fundraiser must possess excellent communication skills to communicate the fundraising initiative systematically to the donors. The candidate must identify, analyze, and realize the power of communication skills while fundraising. Proper communication skills will help cultivate, build connections and sustain long-term relations with the donors.

## Using the "Why?"

Understanding the cause and purpose of the organization is crucial to achieve the desired fundraising results. The candidate must recognize the Why of the nonprofit organization, which becomes the foundation of the fundraising efforts. Therefore, while communicating with the donors, activate their interest in the Why by stating its relevancy and core objective.

# Value Proposition

The unique benefit or solution that a nonprofit organization can offer to potential donors or investors. Fundraisers should clearly articulate their organization's value proposition in order to effectively communicate with donors and secure support.

# Vanity Metrics

Superficial metrics such as social media likes or website traffic that may not necessarily indicate fundraising success. Fundraisers should be cautious of relying too heavily on vanity metrics and instead focus on metrics that measure tangible impact.

# Vendor Management

The process of managing relationships with vendors or external service providers that are contracted to support fundraising efforts. This may include negotiating contracts, monitoring vendor performance, and ensuring effective communication.

## Venture Capital

A type of private equity financing which is provided by investors to startup companies with potential for growth. Fundraisers may be involved in pitching to venture capitalists in order to secure funding for their nonprofit organization.

## Verification

The process of verifying the legitimacy and accountability of a nonprofit organization before making a donation or investment. Fundraisers should ensure that their organization has proper documentation and financial transparency to build trust with potential supporters.

## Visibility

The extent to which a nonprofit organization is seen and heard by their target audience. Fundraisers may need to focus on increasing visibility through strategies such as public relations, social media, and awareness campaigns.

# Vision Statement

A concise and inspiring statement that outlines an organization's long-term goals and aspirations. Fundraisers should understand and embody their organization's vision in order to effectively communicate with stakeholders and inspire support.

# Vital Signs

Key performance indicators or metrics that are used to assess the overall health and success of a nonprofit organization. Fundraisers should be familiar with vital signs and use them to inform fundraising strategies and decision-making.

# Volunteer Management

The process of recruiting, training, and managing volunteers to help with fundraising efforts. This includes establishing volunteer schedules, coordinating with other staff members, and ensuring volunteer satisfaction and retention rates.

# Volunteer Retention

The process of keeping volunteers engaged and committed to an organization's cause over time. Fundraisers may need to develop creative strategies to retain volunteers, such as recognizing their contributions and providing meaningful opportunities for involvement.

# Wealth Screening

The process of analyzing financial records to determine a person's wealth and capacity for giving. This information can help fundraisers target their efforts and prioritize potential donors. It's important to understand the ethical considerations surrounding wealth screening and to ensure that it is done in compliance with regulations.

# Web Analytics

The practice of analyzing data from website usage to track visitor behavior and measure the success of fundraising campaigns. Fundraisers who are skilled in web analytics can use this data to adjust strategies and optimize marketing efforts.

# Well-Connected

Having a network of influential and like-minded individuals who can support fundraising efforts. Being well-connected can help fundraisers gain access to potential donors and generate buzz for events and campaigns.

# Winning Attitude

A positive and persistent mindset that is focused on achieving goals and overcoming challenges. Demonstrating a winning attitude during an interview can show potential employers that you have the drive and determination to succeed as a fundraiser.

# Work Environment

The culture and dynamics of the workplace can significantly impact job satisfaction and success. Understanding the work environment of a prospective fundraiser job can help you determine if it's a good match for your personality and work style.

# Workflow

The series of steps involved in completing a project or task. Understanding the workflow of a fundraising job can help you stay organized and efficient.

# Working Knowledge

A practical understanding of the concepts, tools, and techniques that are relevant to fundraising. Having a working knowledge of fundraising best practices and industry trends can help you stand out as a qualified candidate.

# Workload

The amount of work and responsibility that is expected from a fundraiser. The workload may include researching potential donors, designing and implementing fundraising campaigns, organizing events, and communicating with donors. It's important to ask about workload expectations during an interview to ensure that you can handle the demands of the job.

# Writing Samples

Examples of your past writing projects that can demonstrate your skills and style as a fundraiser. Providing writing samples during an interview can help potential employers evaluate the quality of your work and determine if you're a good fit for the job.

# Writing Skills

The ability to effectively communicate ideas and values through written materials is important for fundraisers. This includes crafting compelling grant proposals, writing engaging social media posts, and creating informative newsletters. Demonstrating strong writing skills during an interview can set you apart from other candidates.